HOW TO' SURF BETTAH

WIT' PALAKA JOE

AN' NO TEEZ DA SPELLING!

by Patrick Ching and Jeff Pagay
Introduction by Brian Keaulana

ALOHA, I'm Brian Keaulana.

It's me, Hawaiian Waterman Brian Keaulana. My ancestors have been riding the surf of Hawai'i for many centuries. My **'Ohana** (family) knows that the ocean is alive and we are part of it. We are fortunate to live in the land of clear and colorful water.

Surfing is such great exercise for our mind, body and spirit (**Lokahi**). Learning to surf can be tough, but it is so rewarding. Knowledge is one of the greatest treasures to give. This book is one of my favorite gifts to those who want to learn **"How Fo' Surf Bettah."** The instruction is good and simple. Plus, I love the local humor. Have fun in learning 'cause in the ocean, the *"Mo' you know the mo' fun you goin' have."*

So, enjoy your adventure. Be respectful and gracious to the sea and your fellow surfers.

Mahalo

FOR FREE SURF FLICK: FLICK PAGE CORNERS FROM BACK TO FRONT!

HOWZIT!!?

I'M PALAKA JOE.

Y'KNOW, THERE'S NOTHIN' LIKE DA FEELIN' OF BEING CARRIED ACROSS THE OCEAN'S SURFACE BY A WAVE. FEW THINGS CAN BRING YOU MORE EXCITEMENT, TRANQUILITY, AND GRATIFICATION THAN SURFING. HAVING GROWN UP IN THE HAWAIIAN SURF, I'VE ACQUIRED THE ATTITUDE AND SKILLS WHICH ENABLE ME TO TEACH THE ART OF SURFING TO EVEN THE MOST HOPELESS LŌLŌS.

I'LL TRY TO SPEAK GOOD ENGLISH, BUT IF I GET CARRIED AWAY, TRY TO UNDERSTAND, I BEEN TALKING LIKE DIS MA' WHOLE LIFE. THERE'S A GLOSSARY IN BACK IF YOU' REALLY CLUELESS.

YOU KNOW, WITH ALL SURFING HAS TO OFFER, DA TING I LIKE MOST ABOUT IT IS

...ONLY GET ONE RULE...

SURF INSTRUCTA'

SO YOU WANNA LEARN HOW FO' SURF BETTAH?

WELL, BEFORE WE PADDLE OUT IN THOSE
TWENTY FOOTERS, LET'S BACK UP A BIT AND
LEARN SOMETHING ABOUT WHAT WE'RE GETTING INTO...

THE HAWAIIAN WORD FOR SURF IS **NALU.** BOARD SURFING, OR **HE'E NALU,**
WAS PIONEERED IN HAWAI'I HUNDREDS OF YEARS AGO. IT WAS THE FAVORITE
SPORT OF MANY HAWAIIAN CHIEFS INCLUDING KAMEHAMEHA THE GREAT.
SINCE THEN, SURFING HAS BECOME POPULAR WORLDWIDE BUT HAS RETAINED
THE REPUTATION AS "THE SPORT OF KINGS." INDEED, GLIDING EFFORTLESSLY
ALONG THE FACE OF A WAVE CAN MAKE ANYONE FEEL LIKE ROYALTY!

PAPA HE'E NALU IS THE HAWAIIAN NAME FOR SURFBOARD. IN ANCIENT TIMES THE BOARDS WERE MADE FROM VARIOUS WOODS INCLUDING 'ULU (BREADFRUIT), **KOA** (ACACIA), AND THE MOST PRIZED **WILIWILI** (HAWAIIAN CORAL TREE). SOME OF THOSE BOARDS MEASURED NEARLY TWENTY FEET LONG AND WEIGHED ALMOST 200 POUNDS!

THE GREAT WATERMAN, DUKE KAHANAMOKU, MADE LEGENDARY RIDES USING A STREAMLINED VERSION OF THE ANCIENT BOARDS. THESE BOARDS WERE USUALLY SHAPED OUT OF HOLLOWED OUT REDWOOD TREES AND WEIGHED ABOUT 50 POUNDS.

THE DAWN OF MODERN SURFING BEGAN IN THE 1940S WITH THE INTRODUCTION OF BALSA AND FIBERGLASS BOARDS FITTED WITH A FIN OR "SKEG." THESE WERE FOLLOWED IN THE LATE 1950S BY FOAM AND FIBERGLASS BOARDS WHICH ARE THE STANDARD TODAY. THESE NEW BOARDS ENABLE RIDERS TO MANEUVER THROUGH WAVES LIKE NEVER BEFORE.

KAMEHAMEHA

DUKE

JOE

THE BEST PART IS THESE BOARDS WEIGH LESS THAN A NĀNĀKULI ROOF-RAT!

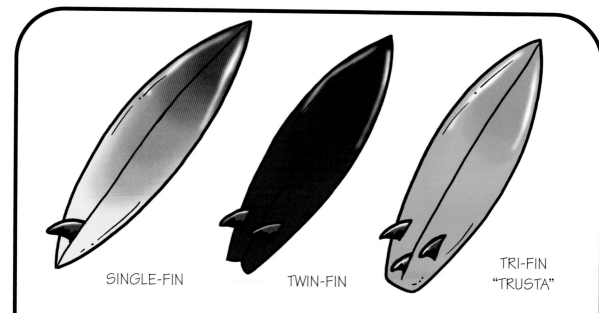

SINGLE-FIN   TWIN-FIN   TRI-FIN "TRUSTA"

RECENT DECADES HAVE WITNESSED DRASTIC CHANGES IN SURFBOARD DESIGN. VARIATIONS IN SHAPES, ALONG WITH FIN SIZE AND NUMBER OF FINS, HAVE REVOLUTIONIZED THE SURFING INDUSTRY.

BY RIDING VARIOUS KINDS OF BOARDS YOU WILL DISCOVER WHAT SHAPES AND SIZES WORK BEST FOR YOU. WHO KNOWS, MAYBE SOMEDAY YOU'LL BE SHAPING YOUR **OWN** CUSTOM BOARDS.

PARTS OF A SURFBOARD

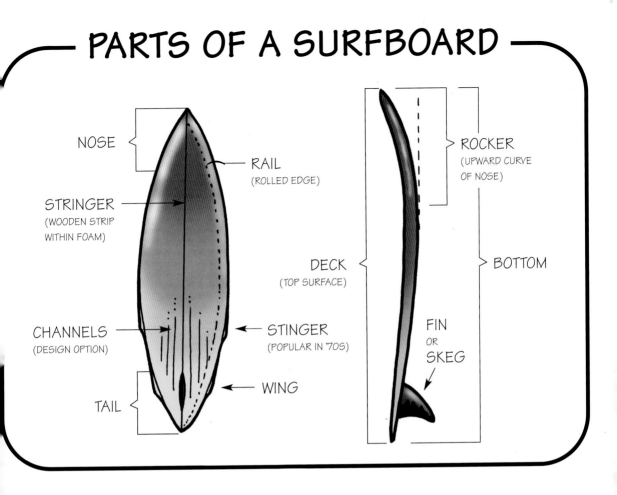

NOSE

RAIL
(ROLLED EDGE)

STRINGER
(WOODEN STRIP
WITHIN FOAM)

CHANNELS
(DESIGN OPTION)

STINGER
(POPULAR IN '70S)

TAIL

WING

ROCKER
(UPWARD CURVE
OF NOSE)

DECK
(TOP SURFACE)

BOTTOM

FIN
OR
SKEG

NOSE AND TAIL SHAPES

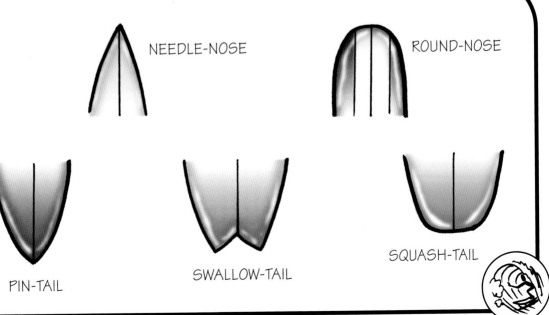

NEEDLE-NOSE

ROUND-NOSE

PIN-TAIL

SWALLOW-TAIL

SQUASH-TAIL

SURF GEAR

BOARD RACKS — MAY BE BUILT, BOUGHT OR BORROWED.
HINT: *DON'T FORGET TO STRAP THEM O*

CAR — *ANY MAKE, MODEL OR CONDITION WILL DO. DOORS AND ROOF OPTIONAL.*

K·DEN

JUGS OF WATER — *FOR DRINKING, WASHING STUFF OFF, OR REFILLING RADIATORS.*

H2O H2O

WAX — *THIS HELPS YOU TO STICK TO YOUR SURFBOARD. RUB IT ON YOUR BOARD — NOT YOUR BODY.*

GLASSES — *ANY KINE AWRIGHT. WHATEVER MAKES YOU LOOK COOL.*

SURFBOARD — *ESSENTIAL EQUIPMENT FOR BOARD SURFING.*

LEASH, CORD — *KEEPS BOARD FROM GETTING SWEPT IN AFTER A WIPEOUT. ALSO HELPS TO LOCATE MISSING SURFERS.*

SHO'TS (shorts) — *STYLES COME AND GO. WARNING: GET THE KIND THAT STAY ON.*

SLIPPA'S — *IN HAOLE: THONGS, SHOES, FLIP FLOPS, SLAPS. WHATEVA', PUT 'EM ON YO' FEET.*
*IT IS CUSTOMARY TO REMOVE SLIP-PA'S BEFORE ENTERING OCEAN.

MUTT — *SOMETHING TO PROTECT YOUR GEAR, ATTRACT BABES, AND EAT LEFTOVERS.*

ANATOMY

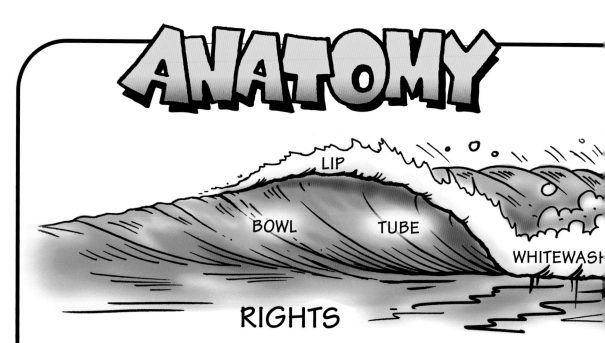

RIGHTS

MOST WAVES ARE GENERATED BY STORMS OUT AT SEA. THE WAVES TRAVEL ACROSS THE OCEAN IN GROUPS OR **"SETS."** AS THE SETS OF WAVES REACH SHALLOW WATER THEY PITCH OUT OR **"BREAK."**

JUST BEFORE A WAVE BREAKS IT IS AT ITS HIGHTEST POINT OR **"PEAK."** DA **"LIP"** IS THE EDGE OF THE WAVE THAT IS IN THE PROCESS OF THROWING OVER. DA **"PIT"** IS WHERE THE LIP IS LANDING. IT IS THE MOST DANGEROUS PART OF THE WAVE. AS IT THROWS OVER, THE WAVE MAY FORM A **"TUBE."**

THE **"WHITEWASH"** IS ANY PART OF THE WAVE THAT HAS ALREADY BROKEN. THE **"SHOULDER"** IS LOCATED AT THE END OF THE WAVE THAT HAS NOT BROKEN. IN SOME LOCATIONS A **"BOWL"** IS FORMED BETWEEN THE TUBE AND THE SHOULDER OF A WAVE. A GOOD EXAMPLE OF THIS IS THE FAMOUS "ALA MOANA BOWL."

OF A WAVE

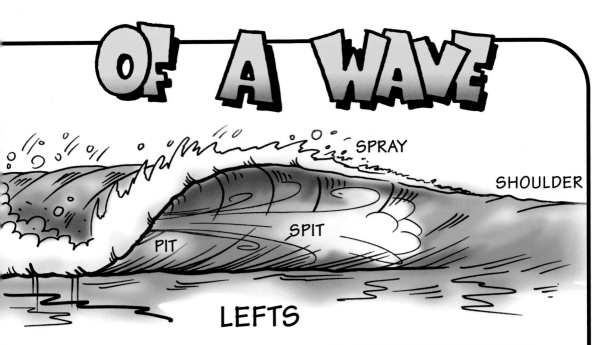

SPRAY

SHOULDER

SPIT

PIT

LEFTS

THE SPEED AND DIRECTION OF THE WIND WILL DETERMINE THE **"CONDITIONS"** IN WHICH A WAVE BREAKS. LIGHT **"OFFSHORE WINDS"** PRODUCE A **"GLASSY"** SURFACE AND FORM NICE HOLLOW TUBES. STRONG **"ONSHORE WINDS"** WILL CREATE **"CHOPPY"** CONDITIONS TURNING THE WAVES TO **"MUSH."**

THE DIRECTION OF A WAVE IS DETERMINED BY WHICH WAY IT BREAKS AS YOU FACE TOWARD SHORE. IF YOU'RE LOOKING AT THE WAVES **FROM** SHORE, JUS' REMEMBER THAT **LEFTS IS RIGHT** AND **RIGHTS IS LEFT**.

IN HAWAI'I, WAVES ARE OFTEN REFERRED TO AS **"BREAKS." "FIRST BREAKS"** ARE THE FARTHEST OUT WHILE **SECOND, THIRD** OR **"INSIDE BREAKS"** ARE CLOSER TO SHORE.

WHEN A WAVE BREAKS, ITS FRONT OR **"FACE"** MAY BE TWICE AS TALL AS ITS **"BACK."** HERE IN HAWAI'I, WE JUDGE THE SIZE OF A WAVE BY THE HEIGHT OF ITS BACK. SO A THREE FOOT WAVE MAY HAVE A FACE MEASURING SIX FEET HIGH.

PEAK

3 ft. back

6 ft. face

REEF

ARE YOU READY FOR YOUR FIRST LESSON IN SURFING?

= EH LŌLŌ, MAKE SURE YOU CAN SWIM FIRST AH!

FIRST TIME SURFERS ARE OFTEN SURPRISED AT HOW HARD IT IS JUST TO SIT ON A SURFBOARD. (SHORTER BOARDS ARE ESPECIALLY SQUIRMY.)
AT FIRST, JUST TRY TO FIND YOUR SPOT IN THE SITTING POSITION. AFTER A WHILE YOU'LL FEEL MORE COMFORTABLE AS YOUR BODY BEGINS TO DISCOVER THE MOST IMPORTANT THING ABOUT SURFING... **BALANCE.**

MANY WOULD BE SURFERS NEVER GET PAST THE LEARNING STAGE BECAUSE OF THE EMBARRASSMENT. PUT IT ASIDE! REMEMBER, EVERYBODY WHO SURFS WAS A BEGINNER AT ONE TIME.

THEN THERE'S THE PAIN. EVEN AN OLYMPIC ATHLETE WILL FEEL HIS MUSCLES TIGHTEN AND BURN IF HE ISN'T USED TO PADDLING A SURFBOARD.

MY BEST WORD OF ADVICE TO THE NOVICE IS, **"ENDURE."**
THE MUSCLE ACHE AND BOARD RASH WILL FADE AND A STRONGER YOU WILL EMERGE **IF** YOU HAVE THE DETERMINATION TO ENDURE THE FIRST FEW SESSIONS.

YAH, I REMEMBA' WHEN I FIRST TRIED TO SURF...

PROPER PADDLING POSITION

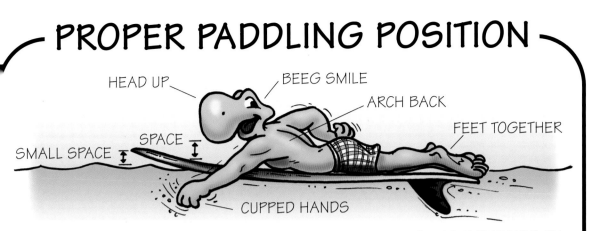

HEAD UP · BEEG SMILE · ARCH BACK · FEET TOGETHER · SPACE · SMALL SPACE · CUPPED HANDS

WHEN PADDLING, REMEMBER TO ARCH YOUR BACK AND POSITION YOURSELF ON YOUR BOARD SO THAT THE NOSE IS BARELY OVER THE WATER. THE POSITION SHOWN ABOVE WILL GIVE YOU THE MOST SPEED WHILE USING THE LEAST AMOUNT OF ENERGY.

PRACTICE PADDLING OUT AND CATCHING WHITEWASH WAVES BACK TO SHORE ON YOUR BELLY. THIS WILL HELP YOU TO FIND YOUR SPOT ON THE BOARD. YOU WILL SEE THAT WHEN YOU ARE TOO FAR FORWARD YOU WILL NOSE DIVE OR **"PEARL"** IN FRONT OF THE WAVE. IF YOU ARE TOO FAR BACK YOU CANNOT GET INTO THE WAVE AND IT WILL PASS YOU BY.

CAUTION: AT THIS STAGE OF LEARNING YOU ARE AT YOUR MOST VULNERABLE AND MOST DANGEROUS STAGE OF THE GAME. BE EXTRA CAREFUL TO AVOID DANGEROUS SITUATIONS. LEARNING IS BEST DONE IN UNCROWDED SURF. USING A SOFT SURFBOARD WILL FURTHER LESSEN THE CHANCE OF INJURY TO YOURSELF AND OTHERS.

WHEN PADDLING BACK OUT

TRY AS MUCH AS POSSIBLE TO STAY CLEAR OF THE BREAKING WAVES. THIS IS TO AVOID INCOMING SURFERS AND ALSO TO KEEP FROM GETTING PUSHED BACK TO SHORE. OF COURSE, YOU CAN'T PADDLE AROUND EVERY WAVE.

SO WHAT HAPPENS WHEN A WAVE BREAKS IN FRONT OF YOU?

DO YOU THROW YOUR BOARD ON THE SIDE AND DIVE FOR DA REEF? YOU COULD, BUT THAT CAN BE DANGEROUS AS WELL AS FOOLISH. SOONER OR LATER YOU GOTTA LEARN TO **"DIP"** UNDER THE WAVES. HERE'S THREE EASY STEPS TO FOLLOW...

DA DIP

STEP 1) *AS THE BREAKING WAVE APPROACHES, PADDLE HARD STRAIGHT TOWARD IT. WHEN THE WAVE IS JUST A FEW FEET IN FRONT OF YOU, GRAB THE NOSE OF YOUR BOARD WITH BOTH HANDS AND PUSH IT UNDER THE WAVE AS HARD AS YOU CAN.*

STEP 2) *ONCE THE NOSE IS SUBMERGED, IMMEDIATELY PUSH THE TAIL OF THE BOARD DOWN WITH ONE OF YOUR FEET. NOW YOUR BOARD AND BODY ARE TOTALLY SUBMERGED.*

STEP 3) *WHEN THE WAVE PASSES OVER YOU, POINT THE NOSE UP TOWARD THE SKY, POP OUT THE BACK, AND CONTINUE PADDLING.*

GETTING UP

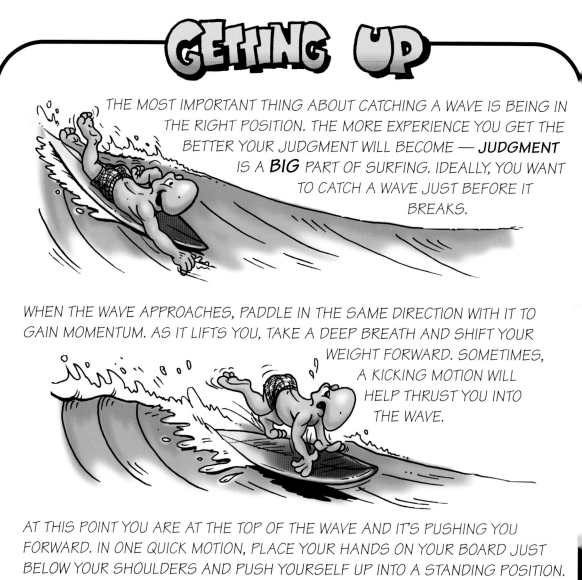

THE MOST IMPORTANT THING ABOUT CATCHING A WAVE IS BEING IN THE RIGHT POSITION. THE MORE EXPERIENCE YOU GET THE BETTER YOUR JUDGMENT WILL BECOME — **JUDGMENT** IS A **BIG** PART OF SURFING. IDEALLY, YOU WANT TO CATCH A WAVE JUST BEFORE IT BREAKS.

WHEN THE WAVE APPROACHES, PADDLE IN THE SAME DIRECTION WITH IT TO GAIN MOMENTUM. AS IT LIFTS YOU, TAKE A DEEP BREATH AND SHIFT YOUR WEIGHT FORWARD. SOMETIMES, A KICKING MOTION WILL HELP THRUST YOU INTO THE WAVE.

AT THIS POINT YOU ARE AT THE TOP OF THE WAVE AND IT'S PUSHING YOU FORWARD. IN ONE QUICK MOTION, PLACE YOUR HANDS ON YOUR BOARD JUST BELOW YOUR SHOULDERS AND PUSH YOURSELF UP INTO A STANDING POSITION.

ONLY EASY!

IT MAY TAKE MANY TRIES BEFORE YOU CAN STAND ON A SURFBOARD WITHOUT FALLING OFF. **KEEP TRYING.** "GETTING UP" ON A SURFBOARD WILL BE ONE OF THE GREATEST ACHIEVEMENTS IN YOUR LIFE!

CORRECT   JUNK

*BE SURE TO STAND WITH ONE FOOT FORWARD AND ONE BACK.
HAVING BOTH FEET SIDE BY SIDE WILL GIVE YOU POOR BALANCE.

PLUS YOU GOIN' LOOK STUPID!!

IF YOU PLACE YOUR LEFT
FOOT FORWARD YOU ARE A
REGULAR FOOT.

IF YOU PLACE YOUR RIGHT
FOOT FORWARD YOU ARE A
GOOFY FOOT.

THE ART OF

THOUGH THE GOAL IN SURFING IS NOT TO **"WIPE OUT,"** IT IS OF COURSE, INEVITABLE. JUST CONSIDER IT PART OF PAYING YOUR DUES. WIPING OUT IS NOT NECESSARILY A BAD THING. IF YOU CAN LEARN TO ENJOY IT YOU WILL ACQUIRE A WEALTHY SOUL.

THE FORCE OF A WAVE CAN HOLD YOU UNDER WATER FOR WHAT SEEMS LIKE AN ETERNITY. YOU FEEL HELPLESS LIKE A SPECK OF SAND IN A WASHING MACHINE. BUT EH, **DON'T PANIC!**

WIPING OUT

IN REALITY YOU CAN HOLD YOUR BREATH LONGER THAN MOST ANY WAVE CAN HOLD YOU UNDER. JUST KEEP YOUR SENSES AND **GO WITH THE FLOW.** SCRAMBLING FOR THE SURFACE WHILE THE WAVE IS STILL CHURNING WILL ONLY WASTE YOUR VALUABLE OXYGEN.

REMEMBER, LET THE WAVE TAKE YOU AND KNOW THAT WHEN IT LETS GO YOU **WILL SURVIVE.** *BUT IF YOU DIE, CAN I HAVE YO' BOARD?*

DIS IS IT! DA MOST CRITICAL PART OF A RIDE. THE OJBECT IS TO GET FROM THE TOP OF THE WAVE TO THE BOTTOM. IF YOU'RE STILL STANDIN'... YOU'VE MADE DA DROP. EVERY MOVE FROM HERE ON IS JUST A MATTER OF SHIFTING YOUR WEIGHT.

BOTTOM TURN

JES' DIG IN AN' GO!

HIT DA LIP

AN AGGRESSIVE TURN OFF THE TOP.

CUT BACK

SWING IT AROUND AND GO BACK FOR MORE.

SPEND AS MUCH TIME IN HERE AS YOU CAN. SCREAM A LOT — IT SOUNDS NEAT!

FLOATER

WHILE COASTING OVER A BROKEN SECTION OF WAVE...THINK LIGHT.

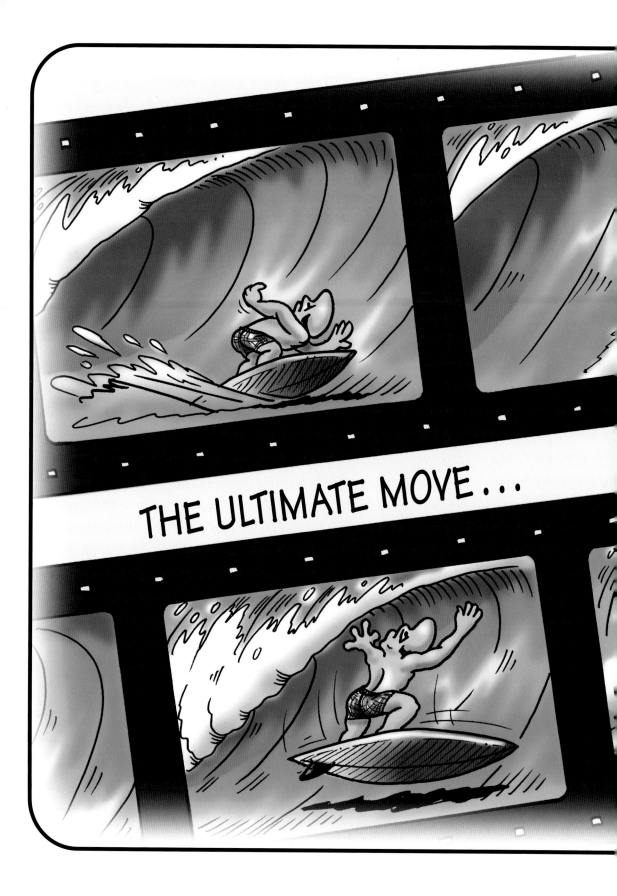

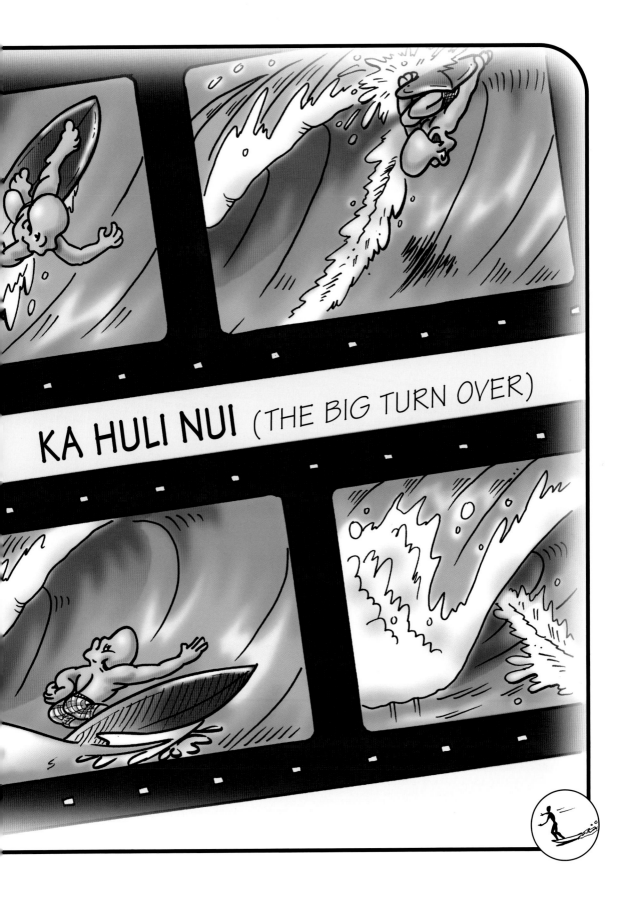

KA HULI NUI (THE BIG TURN OVER)

ANCIENT

A REBIRTH OF ANCIENT STYLES OF SURFING HAS EMERGED IN RECENT YEARS. MANY MODERN SURFERS HAVE DIFFICULTY IMAGINING HOW THESE SOLID WOODEN, SKEGLESS BOARDS WERE MANEUVERED.

OLO SURFBOARDS WERE THE LARGEST BOARDS, SOMETIMES MEASURING TWENTY FEET IN LENGTH AND UP TO 6" THICK. IN ANCIENT TIMES, THESE WERE RESERVED FOR USE BY ALI'I (ROYALTY).

ALAIA BOARDS WERE THE MOST WIDELY USED BY THE COMMON PEOPLE IN ANCIENT TIMES. THEY ARE ABOUT SIX TO TEN FEET LONG AND RELATIVELY THIN.

STYLES

KIKO'O BOARDS WERE THIN LIKE ALAIA BUT QUITE A BIT LONGER (UP TO 18 FEET). THEY WERE PREFERRED IN ROUGHER SURF.

IN DA BEGINNINIG...

BODY SURFING

THE OLDEST AND MOST BASIC FORM OF SURFING IS USING YO' BODY. BODY SURFING REQUIRES YOU TO CATCH THE WAVE JUST AS ITS BREAKING. THE USE OF FINS REALLY HELPS A BODY SURFER **"GET INTO"** A WAVE.

CANOE SURFING

PEOPLE TRAVELING IN CANOES WELCOMED AND ENJOYED **"THE FOLLOWING SEA."** IN UDDA WERDS, THEY LOVE TO CATCH WAVES. WAVES COMING FROM BEHIND THE CANOE HELPED PROPEL THEM TOWARD THEIR DESTINATION.

PLUS, ITS GOOD FUN!

PAIPO BOARDS WERE SHORT (THREE TO SIX FEET), FLAT, WOODEN BOARDS RIDDEN ON ONE'S BELLY. BASICALLY, THE ORIGINAL VERSIONS OF THE SOFT BODY BOARD.

BODY BOARDS OF TODAY ARE MADE OF LIGHT, FLEXIBLE FOAM AND PLASTICS. MODERN BODY BOARDERS DO AMAZING ACROBATIC MANEUVERS BY USING THE POWER OF THE WAVES TO PROPEL THEM THROUGH AIR AND SEA. BODY BOARDS ARE RIDDEN ON THE BELLY, ONE KNEE OR BOTH KNEES, AND EVEN ON ONE'S FEET.

KITE SURFING TOOK WINDSURFING ONE STEP FARTHER. A PARACHUTE TYPE SAIL
OR **"KITE"** CARRIES THE KITESURFER ACROSS THE WAVES
AND OFTEN GETS SOME SERIOUS *"AIR."*

TOW IN SURFING

SOME SURFING DAREDEVILS REALIZED THAT THE LIMITATION OF BIG WAVE SURFING WAS THAT THEY COULD SURF WAVES BIGGER THAN THEY COULD ACTUALLY PADDLE INTO ON THEIR OWN. WITH THE USE OF A JETSKI, SURFERS COULD BE TOWED INTO WAVES AT A HIGHER SPEED, AND THUS THEY ARE NOW ABLE TO *"GET INTO"* HUGE WAVES WELL BEFORE THEY ACTUALLY BREAK OVER.

STAND UP PADDLE

THIS INTERNATIONALLY GROWING SPORT HAS ITS ROOTS IN ANCIENT HAWAI'I. ITS RESURGENCE BEGAN IN THE 1960S WHEN IT WAS PRACTICED BY THE WAIKIKI BEACH BOYS TO KEEP AN EYE ON THEIR SURFING STUDENTS. LONG BOARDS WERE USED WITH THE HELP OF A LONG CANOE PADDLE. FROM THE HIGHER VANTAGE POINTS, THE BEACH BOYS COULD SEE INCOMING SWELLS, GIVE TIPS ON TECHNIQUES, AND EVEN TAKE PICTURES OF THEIR STUDENTS. STAND UP PADDLE SURFING IS A SOURCE OF GREAT EXERCISE AND ENJOYMENT.

SURF

KNOW YOURSELF

LOOK IN DA MIRROR. WHAT DO YOU SEE? BE TRUTHFUL TO YOURSELF ABOUT YOUR SKILLS AND ABILITIES. IF YOU'RE A BEGINNER, **DON'T** CHARGE BIG SURF AFTER WATCHING A **SURF MOVIE!** PUTTING YOURSELF IN SURF ROUGHER THAN YOU CAN HANDLE ENDANGERS YOU **AND** THE FOLKS TRYING TO SAVE YOU.

KNOW YOUR SURF SPOT

BE **AWARE** OF THE PARTICULAR HAZARDS OF YOUR SURF SPOT. KNOW THE REEF, ROCKS, CURRENTS, AND CREATURES OF THE AREA.

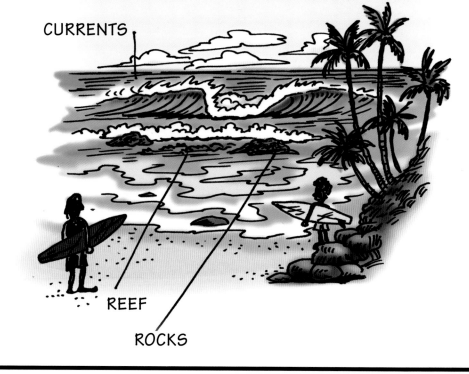

CURRENTS

REEF

ROCKS

SAFETY

KNOW THE TIDES AND SURF FORECASTS

HAVE AN **IDEA** OF WHAT TO EXPECT THROUGHOUT YOUR SURF SESSION. IF THE TIDE IS RISING, IT MAY GET ROUGHER. SURF HEIGHTS CAN RISE **FAST**. A FALLING TIDE CAN **ALSO** LEAVE YOU STRANDED...

WHAT A LŌLŌ

BE ALERT!

KEEP AN EYE ON WHAT YOU'RE DOING AND **BOTH** EYES ON THE WAVES. GOOD SURFERS KNOW WHAT'S HAPPENING **ALL** AROUND THEM. DON'T GET DISTRACTED BY SOMETHING SHINY!

LONGBOARDING

THIS APPROACH TO SURFING ALLOWS FOR CREATIVE EXPRESSION THAT IS NOT AVAILABLE TO SHORTBOARDERS. LONGBOARDS ARE MORE BUOYANT AND STABLE, THEREBY ALLOWING SURFERS TO BE MORE CREATIVE IN THEIR MANEUVERS. "WALKING THE BOARD," "HANGING TEN" AND "TANDEM" SURFING ARE JUST A FEW MOVES POSSIBLE ON LONGER BOARDS.

SURF EDAKET

SURFING HAS MANY UNWRITTEN LAWS. UNFORTUNATELY, EACH SURFER MUST DISCOVER THESE LAWS FOR HIMSELF... THEY ARE, AFTER ALL, UNWRITTEN.

UNWRITTEN LAWS OF SURFING

LAW #1)

LAW #2)

LAW #3)

LAW #4)

LAW #5) * THIS ONE IS REALLY IMPORTANT

LAW #

I **CAN** TELL YOU THAT IT'S NOT ENOUGH JUST TO KNOW HOW TO SURF. SURVIVING IN THE CROWDED, AND OFTEN COMPETITIVE, SURF REQUIRES AN UNDERSTANDING OF SURFING EDAKET.

BE RESPECTFUL OF YOUR FELLOW SURFERS. WE'RE ALL OUT THERE TO ENJOY DA OCEAN.

IN UDDUH WERDS, YOU GOTTA KNOW HOW FO' ACT! -

THERE'S AN OBVIOUS ORDER IN WHICH SURFERS AT A GIVEN SPOT LINE UP TO AWAIT INCOMING WAVES. USUALLY THE BEST, MOST RESPECTED, OR JUST PLAIN **BIGGEST** SURFERS ARE IN THE BEST POSITION AND THEREFORE GET MOST OF THE WAVES.

BUT RIPPA'S, LET DA GREMMIES CATCH WAVES TOO AH!

ONE IMPORTANT THING TO REMEMBER IS ... WHOEVER STANDS UP FIRST, IN THE MOST CRITICAL PART OF THE WAVE, HAS THE RIGHT OF WAY. IT'S NOT NICE TO TAKE OFF IN FRONT OF (OR "DROP IN" ON) THAT PERSON.

SURF HAZARDS

SUNBURN: *SKIN TURNS RED, HOT, SORE; MAY BLISTER. LIPS MAY CRACK AND EVENTUALLY PEEL OFF.*

TREATMENT: *PREVENTION — USE WATERPROOF SUNSCREEN AND LIP BALM. THE JUICE FROM THE ALOE PLANT IS GREAT FOR SOOTHING BURNS. JES' RUB IT ON.*

BOARD RASH: *IF YOUR SKIN IS NOT USED TO THE FRICTION CAUSED BY SURF WAX, IT WILL TURN RED. YOUR RIBS MAY FEEL BRUISED AS WELL.*

SHORTS RASH: *THE GIRLS DON'T KNOW, BUT THE LITTLE BOYS UNDERSTAND.*

TREATMENT: *THIS WILL FADE AS YOU GET USED TO THE FRICTION. SOAP & WATER OR ALOE MAY HELP.*

WANA: *(VAH-NAH) SEA URCHIN. THE SPINES WILL BREAK OFF IN YOUR FEET IF YOU STEP ON THESE.*

TREATMENT: *URINE. WE'RE NOT SURE HOW IT WORKS, BUT ITS A GREAT WAY TO MEET PEOPLE.*

PO'DAGEE MAN O WAR: *A TYPE OF FLOATING JELLYFISH THAT STINGS REAL BAD.*

TREATMENT: *COVER AFFECTED AREA WITH A PASTE OF MEAT TENDERIZER AND WATER, OR THE WHITE SAP FROM A GREEN PAPAYA. CALL A DOCTOR AND WATCH FOR ALLERGIC REACTION.*

BLACK EYE: MAY BE CAUSED BY CRASHING INTO SOMEONE BIGGER THAN YOU.

TREATMENT: THESE USUALLY FADE IN A WEEK OR SO. ICE AND SUNGLASSES MAY HELP.

SORE MUSCLES: ESPECIALLY NECK, SHOULDER AND BACK. MORE COMMON WITH BEGINNERS.

TREATMENT: TOUGH IT OUT! THE PAIN WILL EASE AS YOUR BODY GETS USED TO TWISTING AND PADDLING.

KAKIOS: (KAH-KEE-OHS) VARIOUS SCRAPES, CUTS AND GASHES ACQUIRED BY BOUNCING OFF DA REEF. A.K.A. REEF RASH.

TREATMENT: CLEAN REEF CUTS WELL, THEY ARE EASILY INFECTED. SEE A DOCTOR.

DINGS: PUKAS OR DENTS IN SURFBOARD FROM CONTACT WITH REEF, BODY PARTS, OTHER BOARDS, OR FORGETTING TO STRAP YOUR BOARD TO THE SURF RACKS.

TREATMENT: CAN BE FIXED WIT FOAM, FIBERGLASS AND RESIN. DO **NOT** CALL A DOCTOR.

WHAT ABOUT SHARKS?

SHARKS LIVE IN THE OCEAN. THEY HAVE FOR MILLIONS OF YEARS. THE ONLY GUARANTEE' WAY TO AVOID SHARKS IS TO STAY OUT OF THE OCEAN.

MOST SHARKS WILL NOT BOTHER HUMANS; HOWEVER, THEY ARE NOTORIOUSLY UNPREDICTABLE. DON'T BELIEVE ANYONE WHO CLAIMS TO KNOW EVERYTHING ABOUT SHARKS.

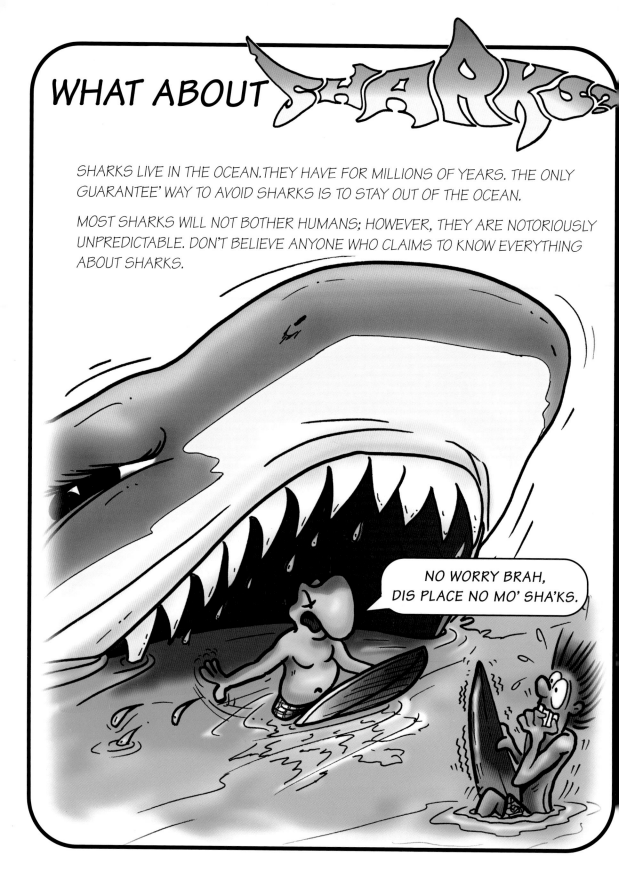

GUIDELINES TO LOWER THE RISK OF SHARK ATTACK:

1) DON'T SURF BEFORE SUNRISE OR AFTER SUNSET.

2) DON'T SURF NEAR RIVER MOUTHS OR HARBOR ENTRANCES.

3) DON'T SURF IN MURKY WATER.

4) DON'T SURF ALONE OR IN SMALL GROUPS.

IN UDDUH WORDS: AVOID ALL THE BEST SPOTS AND CONDITIONS IF YOU' WORRIED ABOUT SHARKS!

AN' DON'T BELIEVE THAT STUFF ABOUT SHARKS ATTACKING SURFA'S 'CAUSE THEY LOOK LIKE TURTLES OR SEALS. I THINK THEY ATTACK TURTLES AND SEALS 'CAUSE THEY LOOK LIKE SURFA'S!

SEAL

TURTLE

SURFA'

SHARK'S EYE VIEW

HOW FO' TALK

(SURF SLANG GLOSSARY)

BAD: GOOD.

BARREL: TUBE, PIPE, THE HOLLOW PART OF A WAVE.

BRAH: SHORT FOR BRUDDUH OR BROTHER. NOT WOMEN'S UNDERWEAR.

DING: PUKA OR DENT IN YOUR BOARD; ALSO, SOUND YOU HEAR BEFORE "DONG."

FRONTSIDE: SURFING WITH THE FRONT OF YOUR BODY TOWARD THE WAVE. OPPOSITE OF BACKSIDE: SURFING WITH YOUR BACK TOWARD THE WAVE.

GONZO: ENTHUSIASTIC, READY FOR ACTION.

GRIND: 1. TO EAT VORACIOUSLY. 2. TO "EAT IT" OR WIPE OUT.

GARENS ALSO **GARENS BALLBARENS:** GUARANTEE(D), A SURE THING.

GREMMIE: GEEK, NURD, IDIOT, OR BEGINNER.

HOO-TA! ALSO **BANZAI!** OR **AHHHH!:** EXCLAMATIONS OF ELATION UTTERED JUST BEFORE TAKE OFF, IMPACT AND/OR POSSIBLE DEATH.

LINE UP: THE TAKE-OFF AREA WHERE SURFERS GATHER TO CATCH WAVES.

LOKOS: REGULARS OR RESIDENTS OF A GIVEN LOCATION OR SURF SPOT.

LŌLŌ: (LOW-LOW) REFERS TO ONE WHO IS NOT ALL THERE. YOU KNOW, LIGHTS ON BUT NOBODY HOME?

MENTO: MENTALLY LACKING, LŌLŌ.

ONREAL: NOT REAL OR SEEMINGLY IMPOSSIBLE.

OVER THE FALLS: TO BE SUCKED UP AND OVER A WAVE THEN DRIVEN UNDER AND SWIRLED AROUND. THIS MAY BE REPEATED SEVERAL TIMES.

PEARL: SHORT FOR "PEARL DIVE;" TO NOSE UNDER AND GRIND ESPECIALLY WHILE TAKING THE DROP.

PO'DAGEE ALSO **POCHO:** PORTUGUESE MAN-O-WAR OR JUST PORTUGUESE IN GENERAL.

PUKA: HOLE, PUNCTURE.

PUMPEN': PUMPING. AS IN "DA WAVES IS PUMPEN'!"

RAD: SHORT FOR RADICAL. SAME AS BAD (MEANING GOOD).

SETS: (NOT SEX!) OFTEN SCREAMED BY SURFERS AS SETS OF WAVES APPROACH.

SIC: SAME AS RAD OR BAD (MEANING GOOD)

SHAKA: AWESOME, RIGHT ON, RIGHTEOUS, FAR OUT AND SOLID.

SHI-SHI: URINE, NUMBER 1.

'KAY-DEN: WELL OKAY THEN, SEE YOU LATER, FAREWELL, THAT'S A WRAP, ALOHA, SAYONADA, DA RIVA DIRTY, I'LL BE DA SAME!

PALAKA JOE'S
WISE WORDS

— *WHERE EVA' YOU STAY... DAS' WHERE YOU ARE...*
  (MAKE THE BEST OF YOUR SITUATION)

— *WHAT EVA' HAPPENS IN DA SURF, YOU **WILL** SURVIVE*
  PROBABLY

  (EVERYTHING WILL BE ALL RIGHT)
  PROBABLY

— *NO PANIC IN DA OCEAN.*
  (KEEP YOUR HEAD — USE IT TO THINK WITH)

— *DA OCEAN IS AN EMPTY CANVAS... NO MO' RULES!*
  (BE CREATIVE... ANYTHING'S POSSIBLE)

— *CLOSE YO' EYE, NO SCA'DE DIE, GOTTA TRY,
  NOT BUMBUY!*
  (NOTHING VENTURED NOTHING GAINED —
  GO FOR IT NOW!)

  AN' LASS BUT NOT LEAST...

  TODAY... IS TOMORROW'S... YESTA'DAY
  (SEIZE THE MOMENT)

DASS DEEP!

AND NOW WATERBUG...

YOU HAVE EVOLVED INTO A BEAUTIFUL WAVE RIDER. I HAVE GIVEN YOU THE KNOWLEDGE YOU NEED TO NAVIGATE YOUR WAY THROUGH THE SETS OF LIFE. IT'S UP TO YOU NOW, WATERBUG. GO. GO AND SEEK OUT THE WAVE OF LIFE. RIDE IT. BECOME ONE WITH IT. NEVER LOOK BACK. THE FUTURE IS IN YOUR HANDS...

START PADDLING!

PATRICK CHING AND JEFF PAGAY

WERE BORN AND RAISED IN HAWAI'I. THEY BEEN BUDDIES SINCE THE SEVENTH GRADE. BOTH GRADUATED FROM MOANALUA HIGH SCHOOL, PATRICK IN 1980, AND JEFF IN 1981. THROUGH THE YEARS THEY BEEN THROUGH COUNTLESS LŌLŌ ADVENTURES, MANY OF WHICH THEY RECORDED AS CARTOONS. THEIR LOVE OF ART, HUMOR, AND OF COURSE SURFING HAS BEEN A COMMON BOND IN THEIR LIVES.

PATRICK HAS BEEN DRAWING PALAKA JOE SINCE THE 2ND GRADE. TODAY HE IS AN INTERNATIONAL ARTIST, AUTHOR AND FOUNDER OF NATURALLY HAWAIIAN GALLERIES. PATRICK TRAVELS WORLDWIDE TEACHING ART AND OF COURSE SURFING. VISIT **PATRICKCHINGART.COM**.

JEFF IS A FREELANCE ARTIST SPECIAL-IZING IN AIRBRUSH ART. HE HAS ALSO PRODUCED MANY CHILDREN'S BOOK ILLUSTRATIONS, WALL MURALS, AND FINE ART CANVASES AND PRINTS. HE ALSO ENJOYS SURFING, BIKING, AND PLAYING GUITAR. VISIT **JEFFPAGAY.COM**

SUPA' GONZO MAHALO

SPECIAL THANKS TO PHILLIS SEGAWA, BARBARA POPE BOOK DESIGN AND MAILE MEYER FOR THEIR CONTRIBUTIONS TO OUR ORIGINAL BOOK "HOW FO' SURF" PUBLISHED IN THE 1980S.

RUTH MOEN DID A WONDERFUL JOB OF UPDATING AND REVISING "HOW FO' SURF BETTAH". SHE ALSO ADDED THE COLOR AND NEW PAGES, AND I LAUGHED OUT LOUD AS I SAW OUR LINE DRAWINGS TAKE ON A NEW COLORFUL LIFE. THANKS TO DALE MADDEN AND ISLAND HERITAGE FOR DOING SUCH A GREAT JOB DISTIRBUTING "HOW FO' SURF" ALL THESE YEARS AND FOR RELEASING "HOW FO' SURF BETTAH" TO A NATIONAL AUDIENCE.

IF DIS BOOK OFFENDS YOU...

RELAX!
IT'S JES' ONE KA'TOON!

IN MEMORY OF RELL SUN WHO DID THE INTRODUCTION TO THE ORIGINAL "HOW FO' SURF" BOOK. RELL HAS BLESSED AND INSPIRED GENERATIONS OF HAWAIIAN SURFERS WITH ALOHA.

IN MEMORY OF FAMILY COURT JUDGE BARRY RUBIN WHO HELPED ME IN MANY WAYS AND GAVE ME THE IDEA TO DO THIS BOOK SO MANY YEARS AGO.

ALOHA,

DEDICATED TO MY PARENTS LARRY AND HELEN PAGAY WHO ARE HOME WITH THE LORD. THEY ENCOURAGED MY ART AND MY SURFING AND STRENGTHENED MY FAITH IN GOD.

YOUR SON,

Published by

ISLAND HERITAGE™
PUBLISHING
A DIVISION OF THE MADDEN CORPORATION

94-411 Kōaki Street, Waipahu, Hawai'i 96797-2806
Orders: (800) 468-2800 • Information: (808) 564-8800
Fax: (808) 564-8877 • islandheritage.com

ISBN 1-59700-920-2
First Edition, Third Printing—2012